Dog Gone Loyalty

BUILDING A LOYAL FOLLOWING

PAUL OSBOURN

iUniverse, Inc.
New York   Bloomington

Dog Gone Loyalty
BUILDING A LOYAL FOLLOWING

iUniverse books may be ordered through booksellers or by contacting:

iUniverse
1663 Liberty Drive
Bloomington, IN 47403
www.iuniverse.com
1-800-Authors (1-800-288-4677)

ISBN: 978-0-595-52130-2 (pbk)
ISBN: 978-0-595-62194-1 (ebk)

Printed in the United States of America

iUniverse rev. date: 1/20/2009

Thanks to my family and friends who encouraged me to write this book, and all the employees, managers and customers that have filled my work world. A special thank you to my wife, the breeder of our dogs, and the puppies that inspired the theme. I am most thankful for the inspiration and wisdom that is given from above, revealed in His Word, a wisdom that never fades and is always confirmed in the truth of our daily life.

CONTENTS

PREFACE

THIS BOOK IS WRITTEN TO provide wisdom and understanding in regard to human loyalty so you can be more effective in securing commitment from those influenced by your leadership. The low level of organizational commitment from employees is a problem many business and institutions find difficult to tackle and one that seems in need of constant attention. There are many writings about loyalty and the benefits of gaining committed followers, but few explore what germinates the emotional seeds of loyalty and how they are groomed and strengthened.

On a recent business trip, I met a gentleman whose story exemplifies the fidelity issue most people in leadership have experienced. We were both heading to Atlanta. He was sitting next to me and began to tell me about his work. He was responsible for setting up large aquariums for a sporting goods chain. I had just been to one of the chain's new stores, and I commented on how impressive the store's aquariums were. He was delighted to explain how the tanks and setup worked. He later said that the store's greatest challenge was keeping cashiers; the turnover had caused many difficulties. His story was no different from hundreds of others I have heard from business leaders. The story goes like this: We tried to do something especially nice one day for the employees. We held a special event to show the employees how much we appreciated them. Unfortunately, some employees complained that it was unfair—they didn't like the food that was served, and the event didn't take their particular tastes and feelings into consideration. The story always ends with the same mysterious questions: why do people act so self-centered, and what do we have to do to keep people committed to our team?

His story and question reminded me of a time when I was put in charge of a small division within a large corporation. This group had historically reported horrible scores on the employee satisfaction survey. I was challenged to turn around the employees' attitudes and improve the satisfaction score. I found myself working with the typical tools provided by human resource departments. The employees and I went through an exercise plotting the personality types in the DISC method. We found we had bankers, artists, drill sergeants, and party animals. We played games in which we were asked as a group to survive a horrible plane crash that supposedly taught us that we were better as a team than we were as individuals. Unfortunately, when we finished the exercises and games, we went back to our individual work islands on the corporate cube farm and quickly forgot the lessons we had taken time to learn. It's one thing to learn lessons from playing a survival game and agreeing as a group to work at applying the concepts, but it's another matter to put the lessons into practice.

The attitudes and thoughts that caused the low satisfaction scores seemed to remain regardless of our efforts. The business had loyalty problems that led to turnover. Poor employee attitudes caused turnover, or folks stayed in body only and were unhappy at work. I concluded that our issues weren't that people didn't believe in team efforts or that managers didn't want to develop committed followers, but instead we lacked an understanding as to how loyalty happens. As the business leader, I tried various ideas that made temporary improvements, but in the end, I found I had nothing more than a few small solutions, not enough to solve a large problem. It was like have a few small pieces to a jigsaw puzzle without the big picture on the box and the larger parts needed to complete the puzzle.

My epiphany came when my wife invited me to participate in one of her life adventures. She wanted to breed our golden retriever with a standard poodle, producing the new superbreed of goldendoodles, that she had researched and studied. This amazingly successful venture gave me a closer look at the canine-human relationship, revealing principles in human loyalty that answered the aquarium manager's questions. The puppy placements allowed me to observe the beginnings of devoted relationships, and in doing so, I began to see foundational components of the obligation sensors in human beings.

Doggone Loyalty examines the one loyal relationship that does not appear to waiver. The old saying about dogs being man's best friend describes one relationship in which commitment and fidelity are strong. I'm not talking about a dog's loyalty to its owner, but rather the loyalty of people to their dogs.

By observing the most loyal of relationships, those between people and their dogs, I developed a sense of what fuels people's allegiance in ways I hadn't encountered in business. I thought to myself that if the trendy corporate off-site retreats, in which a small group of people head out to a place surrounded by nature's beauty, can help upper-level managers better understand themselves, their business, and their relationships, then perhaps what I was seeing could benefit those who lead the masses in similar ways. As I watched people demonstrate their loyalty to their newly adopted puppies, I became more convinced that the relationships between people and their dogs reveal great wisdom about loyalty, an emotion that often is concealed in the workplace.

INTRODUCTION

IN THE SUMMER OF 2007 one of the most unusual loyalty wars took place in American culture. Our love for sports ran into our love for dogs, and the dogs won. One of the National Football League's most popular superstars, Michael Vick, suddenly became one of the most despised athletes in the era of modern sports when he was discovered to be involved with the inhumane treatment of animals. Americans' faithfulness to football and its players had been unmovable—no price was too high for its fans, no crime by a player was unforgivable—until a star player was caught and arrested for his involvement with and funding of criminals who abused and mistreated a group of dogs.

The dogs they mistreated weren't the neighborhood golden retrievers but rather a dog often involved with violent attacks on children, the pit bull terrier. While pit bulls may not be a favorite breed because of their association with attacks on humans, these least-loved canines superseded the loyalty to a pro athlete because the fidelity card of kindness to animals trumped all. Advertisers cancelled commercials, Vick's sponsorships were pulled, and his athletic shoe was discontinued.

The events of the Michael Vick tragedy proved three things: loyalty in America is not dead; Americans' love for and faithfulness to their dogs is one of the deepest forms of loyalty in our country; and understanding and applying the basics of people's allegiance to their dogs can aid leaders in building commitment with those who follow them.

Most leaders at some point have experienced what feels like, at best, follower defection, and at worst, complete betrayal. Those in charge may periodically conclude that loyalty is dead when it comes to the American workplace, but loyalty is not dead. Loyalty may be dormant in various workplaces, but it was on full display in the summer of 2007 and can still be viewed at various sporting, political, and religious events each day.

The intention of this book is to walk leaders through the germination and growth of the dynamics of loyalty, and to provide actions that can create a culture of allegiance among employees or members of their respective organization. *Doggone Loyalty* should be read by anyone who wants to develop a dedicated following. I hope that by applying some dog sense to what is, unfortunately, described as dog-eat-dog world, leaders can be more effective in strengthening the dedication of their followers.

Most business leaders believe if they can strengthen loyalty within the workforce, the improvement will lead to dedicated customers. Frederick Reichheld, the author of the outstanding book *Loyalty Rules*, has written extensively about and proved in numerous case studies the positive effects of committed employees and their impact on customer satisfaction, a major driver of profitability. Reichheld encourages business leaders to understand "that building customer loyalty is limited, unless similar efforts to build employee loyalty are in place, so together a passion for the firm is ignited." [1] Businesses that create, develop, and sustain a culture of employee loyalty provide the soil for customer loyalty to take root.

Yes, you would rather be free to work on ideas and projects that improve the operation's efficiency or grow the business, but you find yourself held back by training and hiring issues. Perhaps you're a manager who was blindsided by a recent employee defection that came without warning, or maybe your employees have reported poor scores on the recent employee satisfaction survey, items all too common in today's business. Perhaps you're simply wondering if loyalty is dead in the workplace and whether anything can be done about it, short of paying everyone like a professional athlete.

Yes, as someone who has walked in your shoes, I wrote this book precisely for people like you who are looking for practical and affordable solutions.

I wrote *Doggone Loyalty* to help mangers and business leaders who are frustrated by the lack of loyalty in the workplace and tired of corporate clichés proposed as solutions. I write from a perspective informed by experience and balance, that of a frontline leader sharing the wisdom learned in twenty years of work and management experience. I also draw on the perspective of my three daughters, who provided insights of young people in the workforce, and my wife, who helped me see a woman's perspective. Most important, I write from the position as one who has walked in the culture described. I am not a PhD writing on a behavioral science theory or a Fortune 500 CEO writing from the inner circle at the top; but rather, I write from an everyman's management perspective that I hope will deliver the mentoring advice that the workplace elders used to deliver at breakfast counters, corner taverns, and Sunday afternoon suppers. I write from practical experience and as an eyewitness who understands that loyalty is elusive and surprisingly shallow in many employees. Like most business owners and managers, I understand the challenge of building commitment from employees with limited resources.

In a February 2005 interview, then Starbucks CEO Jim Donald stated that the turnover rate among Starbucks managers, to be less than half that of the quick-service food industry.[2] One Starbucks executive explained that the high retention rate was due to superior screening and a strong pay and benefits program. While I agree that screening and a good pay plan play a role in retention, I'm convinced that Starbucks and companies that have loyal employees tap into something much deeper than personality selection and payment. Hiring the right people is a great starting point, for new hires, however most managers have to work with whom they have, not whom they hope to have.

This book explores the mysterious emotion of human loyalty and brings to the surface practical applications. *Doggone Loyalty* will not only leave you with a deeper understanding of human loyalty, but it also will equip you with practical ideas and actions that you can apply in any workforce on any budget to effectively improve retention and commitment.

Loyalty is a sense of obligation to remain in a relationship while at the same time maintaining a deep willingness to commit to the value system formed by the relationship. The relationship celebrates both its history and its continuation into the future. In business, the employee-employer commitment must remain strong because competition may at any time seek to raid your talent pool. Loyalty is measured by a person's willingness to enthusiastically follow the leaders' direction. Loyalty occurs when individuals fulfill their emotional needs for power, prestige, and significance, while simultaneously maintaining hope and confidence that their unfulfilled needs will be met because they remain committed to those in charge. Loyalty is driven and sustained by leaders who acknowledge and help their followers move from who they are and where they are to who they want to become and where they want to go. *Doggone Loyalty* is an explanation of how to make that happen.

Although most businesses today may not face the disruptive nature of labor strikes, the same employee frustrations that fuel such movements exist, often damaging morale and creating an apathetic workforce. When these frustrations are left unresolved, a new type of defection often occurs. Your employees may not vote to strike and then protest at the company entrance, as was the case in the first half of the twentieth century, but they vote with their feet. They leave the organization and join another, or they strike by showing up without any commitment or dedication. Feelings of insignificance, poor self-image, and lack of economic progress are often ignored or go unnoticed by those in charge, resulting in a more subtle form of disloyalty among employees that slowly eats away at productivity. The root cause and cure lie in the human spirit's thoughts and emotions regarding loyalty. Those managers who can identify and help resolve these frustrations by giving their followers a true sense of purpose will minimize the negative effect of followers who see no choice but to defect, or show up in body only. I invite you to explore the factors that lead to loyalty so you can be better equipped to strengthen the allegiance of those within your sphere of leadership.

CHAPTER ONE:
THE LEADERSHIP LOYALTY CHALLENGE

"A real leader faces the music, even when he doesn't like the tune."
—Anonymous

HAVE YOU EVER BEEN CONNECTED to a business that decided to invest in new technology, or implement a new procedure, but the resistance from the workers greatly diminished the anticipated return on investment? Have you ever been part of business that was growing rapidly, in need of additional workers to lighten the load, but the new recruits did not stay? Have you ever witnessed customer losses when a key employee, unexpectedly resigns? Perhaps you went to the same hair stylist for months and suddenly your stylist left the salon, leaving you frustrated with a replacement. These challenges and frustrations are all connected to employee loyalty.

Because you're reading this book, you most likely don't need more information on the loyalty problem, but instead you need loyalty solutions. The simple demographic facts tell us, that as the baby boom generation moves into retirement over the next 10 years, the fight for quality workers will intensify. A Google alert on "employee loyalty" or "employee turnover" will fill your inbox with articles about the challenges in retaining workers. What's hard to find are insightful ideas and affordable action plans to help you solve the problem.

The weight of responsibility for keeping good employees tends to rest on managers, as shown by the old saying that most employees do not quit companies; they quit managers. A manager's ability to keep key employees impacts customer retention, innovation and sustain growth. We are relational creatures, and managers are being asked to pay closer attention to commitment and retention, because failing to do so has become more costly. Most managers know that it's easier to manage a business in which the employees and customers are loyal. It is expensive and difficult to find and recruit qualified employees in any labor market.

The typical tactics the average manager may use to create a more positive culture often result in the manager and workers worse off relationally than if the manager had attempted nothing. The office lunch is one such tactic that can drive managers crazy and exemplifies the point.

Let's say the business has a successful month, so the boss buys lunch for the office. Later in the afternoon, someone stops in to advise the boss that the menu selection was not his or her favorite. The next month the business does well again, but this time the boss assigns several employees to handle the luncheon to avoid ordering something the troops don't like. This time after the luncheon, the employees assigned to the task inform the boss they're not interested in doing the planning again because they don't want to deal with the complaints about the menu.

The manager in this type of scenario often feels resentment toward the employees. She or he may ask her- or himself, what must I do, as a manager, for the group to be more positive?

Perhaps a manager decides to provide flexibility in employees' starting and quitting times. The effort to be flexible, however, leads to more requests for more flexibility and an attitude of entitlement. The flexibility offer may upset the frontline supervisor who doesn't like it, or one department can't have the same flexibility and, in turn, complains that the manager is showing favoritism. Quite often, attempts to create a positive place to work end with someone who is unhappy, which causes the efforts to cease.

The complexity of the modern workforce often tempts leaders to employ styles of management that are toxic to loyalty in the workplace. After attempts to be nice have resulted in new dissatisfaction, the typical manager may then shift to Marine commander mode. In this mind-set, the manager tries to crack down with strict discipline, resulting in employee calls to the corporate human resources department or in sharp declines in the ratings on the employee satisfaction survey. Those who take a "my way or the highway" attitude will most likely find that their followers' allegiance not only gets worse, but their time is dominated with policing disciplinary rules.

Managers who move in the opposite reaction and apply the apathy theory of "you can't change City Hall" tend to lead the group into a cluster of apathy, resulting in poor performance, and soon calls for a new manager are made.

It is easy for a manager to slip into negative thinking after trying different strategies and styles. It is tempting for leaders to tell themselves that they're being held responsible for the results but not given the authority to carry it out. Leaders may be right to a certain degree in that assessment, but everyone else in management is facing the same challenge. The person in charge is tempted to believe that no matter what he or she does, the employees are never satisfied.

In a sense, these thoughts of "no matter what you do" are correct because the problem is not what you're doing. The problem is what your workforce is thinking.

The first thing that grabs you regarding the loyalty between people and their dogs is the fact that the relationship has more to do with what the person thinks and feels than what the dog does. This is a radical departure from the way most managers see life and commitment in their organization. By their nature, most managers are fixers. Leaders often see their role as the problem-solver who leads their followers to successful accomplishments. They are the coach who has the play that will work when the team is losing. Managers fix the problem at the restaurant when the meal is bad, and they resolve a host of other situations in business. "Let me talk to the manager" is the customer's cry when a problem arises because managers are perceived as fixers. Interestingly, dogs don't fix anything—they break things—yet people are devoted to their dogs because of how they feel about themselves in the relationship.

The point is not that you should behave like a dog and go chewing up people's paperwork, but if you want to influence your workforce's loyalty, you have to understand that the battle is in the hearts and minds of the followers, not merely in what the boss does or does not do. The hardest thing for a manager to understand is that it's not so much who you are or what you do that matters; it's who the employees think they are that matters. Coaches understand that it's who the player thinks he or she is, in terms of his or her confidence and ability to perform, that matters, more so than who the athlete thinks the coach is. A sports team has to understand its identity before it can relate to the coaches identity. The focus of loyalty and retaining followers is not primarily about who the leaders are, though that is important, but rather it is whom the followers think they are.

Simply put, a leader must first understand his or her followers before the followers can understand their leader. The fixer mind-set mistakenly thinks, with more messages to the workers, via emails and meetings, the workers will become convinced to be loyal to my leadership. Unfortunately, the poor communication processes of most organizations, erodes dedication and allegiance more rapidly. Communication processes tend to accelerate the retention problem because leadership tends to be the messenger, while rarely being the receiver, the listener, or an audience of its followers. The television series *The Office* lampoons the over-communicating manager and is a humorous picture of this problem.

To successfully fill the allegiance vessel of their followers and slow down turnover, managers must understand the basic loyalty sensors that we all have and the starting point is in the followers' thoughts. Three individuals who have developed large loyal followings, by primarily focusing on understanding the concerns and desires of followers, are President Barack Obama, spiritual leader Joel Osteen, and life-coach Steven Covey. These leaders are examples why loyalty is more about the followers thinking, than the leaders actions.

Barack Obama taps into people's desire to improve the nation, as well as themselves, by using inspirational words to motivate them to follow him, but his secret to attracting followers is found in every speech. When he speaks, he almost always mentions a person who has shared with him a problem, demonstrating both his willingness to listen and ability to understand his followers. The follower thinks, this leader understands my pain, he sees my problem, and is now in the right frame of mind to listen and follow. Obama then lays out his political plan in helping people move from where they are to where they want to go. Obama's followers look to him as a political vehicle to help them realize their dreams.

Joel Osteen, a spiritual leader, teaches and guides his followers in closing the gap between who they think they are and who they wish they were, a process that is described in his book, *Become A Better You.*[3] Osteen offers his followers spiritual teachings and principles that close the gaps in their life. The principles are broad and his approach basic, but he is able to help people become the better person they want to be. Osteen also provides key insights into loyalty. He has built one of the largest churches in America, and his books are best sellers.

Stephen Covey, the author of *The 7 Habits of Highly Effective People* and other best sellers, is another example of a person who understands the issue of closing the gap in his follower's minds. Covey, like Osteen, assumes that people recognize the need to be more effective than they are currently. Covey then lays out seven habits of people who are effective, thereby providing a path for people who feel inadequate to follow to become more effective and confident.

The methods described by these leaders may not line up with your beliefs, but millions of people have read these books and follow these leaders because they want to improve their lives. One could debate the validity of the leaders' methods (I will leave that for you to take up); however, people who see their workplace as means to making them a better person also will see it as a place to invest their loyalty. A leader within a workplace or organization who can help people accomplish their desires to be something more will build loyalty in his or her followers. The chapters ahead provide insights for leaders to effectively understand the similar life gaps people are seeking to close at work. The beginning chapters provide insights and actions that can help indentify and bridge the gaps, resulting in deep-seated loyalty. The later chapters advise how to keep it.

Chapter Two:
Why Am I Here? The Privilege Gap

"The person who labors, labors for himself for his hungry mouth drives him."
—Proverbs 16:20

MOST EVERYONE REMEMBERS THEIR FIRST paycheck—both the excitement of earning your own money and the shock of how much was left after taxes. Most of us who worked as teenagers made plans to buy something that we hoped would provide some experience or thrill. The paycheck itself was not our end game, nor was it just receiving the money, but it was a car, camera, concert ticket—some privilege we wanted that required money.

One of the mistakes business leaders make regarding loyalty is assuming that people work for a paycheck. People work for the rights and privileges paychecks bring, not the actual money. The paycheck, which is more often a direct deposit transaction, is access to life experiences, not merely the recording of deposits in a bank account.

Unfortunately, most managers are taught that the almighty dollar is why people show up and is what motivates each person's commitment to the business. In fairness to managers, workers typically tell them they would rather have money than a perk. Ask employees if they would rather have a holiday party or $50, and they will tell you $50. However when it comes to building loyalty, money is rarely listed as the top reason people stay with a job. Here is your first clue to understanding the human emotion of loyalty: people do not always mean what they say. Understanding that a paycheck is the channel by which people receive privileges is key in building loyalty.

If you watched the 2008 presidential primary debates, you saw how the candidates consistently sought followers by promising to fill gaps in the privileges they believed people wanted, yet did not have. Some talked economics, others health care, and others discussed security from terrorism. But each candidate, in a sense, spoke of an increase in privilege that he or she would help provide the electorate.

In our consumer-driven society, the desire for more rights and privilege is an ever-increasing gap and is often a major contributor to workplace turnover. A manager can strengthen allegiance to the company if he or she can show employees how working there provides access to more of the benefits they desire. Managers who help close the gap between the privileges workers possess, and the privileges workers desire, are managers who will build a following. The degree of success depends on the manager's ability to uncover the privileges and gaps with the employees and carefully seek to close them. Watch any investment advisor advertisement and you'll see the point being made: invest with us and get access to more of life's wonderful offerings.

I became keenly aware of this insight while placing dogs with families, in which a significant amount of money was paid.

I observed how unimportant the money was to most people. The rights and experiences the money would bring was the important factor. Not one person ever questioned our price or displayed a reluctance to spend it for our dogs. To this day, we continually receive e-mails and photos about the dogs and the joyful experiences they have brought to the homes they were placed in. One woman who had adopted a dog for her son wrote to tell us her son was so happy with the dog that she received at least fifty hugs since bringing the puppy home. Another set of parents who had been concerned about their college daughter wrote about how much fun their daughter and her sorority sisters were having with the dog. The puppy had changed her college experience for the better, and the parents were less concerned about their daughter. The lesson was obvious: people spent the money in hopes that a puppy would improve the relationships in their lives, through the experiences the puppy would bring.

The reason experiences are more important than money is experiences extend into other realms of life. The benefits, perks, and privileges of working for your company are part of the bragging rights that your workers carry to the neighborhood cookout. It is the next insight I discovered involving people's allegiance sensors. Although I like to believe that the families that purchased our pups were warm, caring families that had the attributes we wanted for our dogs, I'm also sure that each family member enjoyed a little boasting to friends and neighbors about the beautiful new dog they had purchased. The e-mails we receive confirm the observation, because most of the notes mention the positive comments the writer's friends, family members, and neighbors have made about the dogs: "Ruby is the talk of the neighborhood," or "Louis is well-known on the campus. " Every note described the special feeling these dog owners had experienced and how the dog had impacted their world. I'm confident that many purchasers who were parents' were influenced by the anticipated excitement their kids would express in getting a puppy.

You often see a similar phenomenon at work when someone buys a new car and drives it to the office, and everyone goes out to the parking lot to admire the new purchase. People work for the right to experience what money brings to them and their loved ones and for the right to display those privileges to the world. I'm not suggesting people would keep coming to work if you shut off the payroll, but when you begin to explore the question of why people work and discover it's more about the access that money brings, you begin to understand your workforce. This difference is subtle but, at the same time, significant.

I saw families dropping cold, hard cash for dogs that would cost them several hundred dollars per year to feed and take care of. The families really didn't care about the money in their checking account. They cared about bringing home a dog that would love on them and their kids. Money delivers privileges that fill all sorts of emotional holes, such as respect, self-esteem, and status. People work to fulfill feelings found in an experience, which often requires cash to participate. Place a dollar bill in a purse or wallet with other dollar bills, and you can't remember which one it was. The reality is that money, once placed in your life, can't be differentiated from the other money, but the life events that those dollars bring and the feelings that accompany those events will be remembered.

In today's world, the paycheck has almost disappeared; it's been replaced with direct deposit and payroll debit cards. People no longer study their paychecks and examine their take-home pay; instead they focus on the liberties they can afford. Therefore, loyalty requires us to see beyond work as a financial exchange for services on the job.

Because people want life benefits as well as pay, many companies offer their employees special discounts for phone service, banking, and automobile purchases as part of their perks. We're seeing more retailers that offer preferred discounts and services that appeal to a wide base of employees. Recently a men's clothing chain began offering discounts to large corporations that employ significant numbers of professional men. The clothing chain gains access to a desirable customer base, and the employer can help guide dress codes, which have become increasing more difficult to enforce since the implementation of business casual. I know of a trucking firm whose owner invested in vacation properties at which his employees and their families receive discounted accommodations. These special offers and treats keep employees on your team.

Employees are often willing to hang in there longer if they feel they'll lose rewards. Small perks play a role in retaining workers and help strengthen their allegiance.

While leading a company of twenty-five employees, I had purchased small raffle prizes for our annual Christmas party. Somehow we ended up a few prizes short, and two employees didn't get a prize. It was amazing to me that a $10 gift certificate made a difference to people, but it did. I went out the next day and purchased a couple of gift cards for the employees who hadn't received a prize and was amazed to see how much it meant to them. It wasn't the $10 that was important; it was the message that they mattered enough to be included in the perks the others had received.

Managers can often easily fill the gap between the privileges workers currently possess and the privileges they desire by offering local businesses access to your workforce. Quite often retailers are willing to foot the bill for the perks in exchange for the opportunity to do business with your employees. It's a win-win for all participants and a big step to building loyalty.

You don't have to be the head of a big company to make this happen; a local frontline manager can often arrange for discounted perks in the community. As a manager, you may know someone who can give your employees a great deal on their next car, or perhaps a local eatery will provide a 10 percent discount. Depending on the workforce, a company-sponsored membership to Sam's Club or Costco may be the difference in lowering next year's turnover rate.

A business can only pay so much money in wages, but the more you work with employees in closing the gap of privilege, the more loyalty you will find. I knew of a very successful business owner who would buy a new Mercedes every year and would offer someone on the staff a chance to buy her old Mercedes at a significant discount. Within a few years, her parking lot had several luxury cars in it. Through her generous spirit and willingness to close the gap, she had cultivated employees with incredibly deep affection and loyalty to her leadership and business.

Here are few practical, easy-to-implement ideas to fill the privilege gap:

Start by creating a retention budget, and then determine the kinds of perks or rewards that can be handed out. Look for opportunities to leverage the buying power of your workforce, knowing that the smallest group is desirable to some businesses near your company.

Find a car dealership that is close to the office and ask the manager or owner to give your employees discounts for oil changes and invoice pricing on new cars.

If you have a small company, purchase everyone a membership to a local wholesale club store, like Costco or Sam's Club.

Give employees gift cards to restaurants and movie theaters when you think they have performed a task especially well. They will remember it longer than cash or a plaque.

You can create a culture in which workers or followers see that being part of the organization comes with perks that they'll lose if they leave. You don't have to spend a fortune to create loyal feelings, but whatever you do spend will cost far less than the price of turnover. The employees in many of the examples in the chapter receive an increase in purchasing power and prestige without ever increasing the payroll.

CHAPTER THREE:
WHO AM I? THE IMAGE GAP

"As in water face reflects face, So the heart of man reflects man."
—Proverbs 27:19

ONE OF THE AMAZING TRUTHS as to why people follow certain leaders in politics, religion, business, or entertainment is that the followers are often inspired by what the leaders reflects back toward them and their image. Following someone makes a statement about oneself; in doing so, the follower says, "I agree with or am like this particular leader. I support Senator MacGenius because I want people to see me as being intelligent, not just because I think he's smart."

When people came to discuss adopting a dog, they had questions about the parents and the typical questions you would expect in purchasing a dog. However, as we spent time with various families, we found the big question was, "Who does this dog say that I am? Should I become the person that takes it home?"

In the world of goldendoodles, people answered this question with many different answers. Each person was, in part, buying a dog to make a statement about him- or herself. For some folks, the answer involved how the dog reflected the intelligence of their choices. Some stated that they thought goldendoodles were a smart dog that would not shed, showing how smart their selection was. Others were looking for a low allergy–type dog, and for others their choice was based on their sense of style and appearance. But no matter the reason for choosing to adopt a goldendoodle, it was always a statement about them; the dog was simply making the statement. The new owners were filling an image gap—how people saw them and their families and how they wanted themselves and their families to be seen.

A second profound gap a leader needs to understand is the image gap. It is the gulf between what people think their image is and where they would like their image to be. To successfully fill the image gap, you must pay careful attention to understand both the image people currently have of themselves as well as the one they want to have. Leaders who are effective in bridging this gulf can not only strengthen loyalty internally, but they can also effectively recruit highly sought-after candidates who feel misunderstood and stranded in their image at their current position. Image is why Apple Computer stores have a Genius Bar staffed by geniuses, instead of a technical support desk with tech reps, and Starbucks workers are called partners and baristas, instead of cashiers and drink makers.

I was observing a panel on retention in which a couple of truck drivers and managers were talking about what drivers wanted from their companies to keep them loyal. The managers started the conversation as to their thoughts about driver retention. The managers both talked about the typical items you would expect, such as vacation time, pay, and hours worked. Each management person also indicated that no matter what they offered, it did not seem to improve their retention issues. Then the drivers spoke, and each one clearly stated that he wanted to be distinguished and recognized as a quality driver and not lumped in with poor performers. The truckers were telling the leadership on the panel and in the audience that they wanted their company to provide a professional image in exchange for professional performance and commitment. The people behind the wheel wanted their bosses to close the gap from an image of how management and the public typically see them to a desired image of a professional driver. The truck drivers specifically noted that it was upsetting to be lumped together with the general driving population when they saw themselves as drivers of excellence and professional standing. It was a clear case of who they thought they were in the public and management's eyes and wanting something better.

A skilled recruiter from a competitor would have been able to lure these drivers into a lateral move by offering them acknowledgment. This might have consisted of a jacket or shirt that would remind these men, starving to be distinguished, that the best drivers on the road worked for XYZ company and the XYZ managers wanted them because they believed they were the top of the line.

When Bryon Nelson died, the *Dallas Morning News* reported that many professional golfers, including money winner Justin Leonard, remembered Nelson for his letters of encouragement that came at times when they were not playing well. Nelson's letters were notes of encouragement in terms of where these professional golfers saw themselves and where Nelson thought they wanted to be. If players who are good enough to play on the PGA, and win significant amounts of money while playing, appreciate people closing the gap for their perception of self, you can be assured that everyone who works for your company is thankful for encouraging words of assurance. The letters the players described were a perfect example of a leader helping people narrow the gap between the perception the person thought they had and the image the person wanted to project. In the movie *The Replacements*, Gene Hackman plays a coach who tells his quarterback who is trying to make a comeback, "I want you to become the player you are capable of becoming, not the player you are."

The image layer of loyalty in a workplace is created because every employee is a partial reflection of the company's image. Tell someone you work for Apple Computer and they believe you know something about computers, even though you may be an accountant. Businesses have an incredible opportunity to close the image gap in their employees' minds and in turn build loyalty. We are by nature insecure in our image to some degree; even those most comfortable in their own skin want to improve their self-appearance.

Teenagers believe that if they wear a certain brand of jeans, it tells the world they are somebody of significance. Almost everyone is provided a reflection by the car they drive; as the slogan goes, "You are what you drive." A recent advertisement stated that driving a Honda told people that you were smart. There was a time that working for IBM projected an image of being conservative, because the men wore blue suits and white shirts; they were not permitted to wear blue shirts. Some companies have an image of hiring mavericks; others are militaristic. Countless images are given to people because of the companies they work for. Many of my neighbors in suburbia are professionals in various fields during the week, but when they hop on their Harley Davidson motorcycles on the weekend, they become someone else. The Harley Davidson logo or Mercedes Benz logo, and others like them project great meaning.

The challenge employers need to address is convincing their employees that working for their company projects an image of being intelligent, successful, creative, or a similar positive characteristic. Consider that Volvo's logo is the scientific symbol for masculinity and the company is about safety. The BMW logo reflects a propeller blade against a blue sky that was used for military aircraft in Germany. The BMW slogan, "The ultimate driving machine," is all about precision engineering. Employees tend to go negative about their company's image. It only takes a few communication failures and a lost client or two before people begin to perceive that working for their employer is negative. It is human nature to believe the worst. People need management to convince them otherwise.

One way to answer the image question of loyalty is by using *the management mirror*. If you're ever around teenagers, especially teenage girls, they spend a great deal of time in front of mirrors. The teenager is typically insecure about how others will see her, and the mirror is a place that allows her to find reassurance and feedback. Employees in many cases are looking to managers to reflect what their image is in the workplace. Workers are often unsure about what people think of them and how they are perceived. The worst thing management can do is distort the reflection by providing feedback only when something is wrong. The second worst reflection is to not provide one at all. Imagine teenagers in a house without mirrors; they would be using silverware, glass, anything that was shiny to see their reflection. When management fails to provide reflection back to employees, the anxiety levels rise, and the temptation to go negative occurs. Ed Young, the leader of the mega-church Fellowship Church in Grapevine Texas, once asked parents, if you only had mirrors like the type found at fun houses—the mirrors that distort your face and make you short or tall—what kind of confidence would your children possess? What would a mirror that increased teenagers' facial blemishes do to their attitude? When the only feedback that employees receive from leaders focuses on mistakes, you create a distorted image that is not conducive to loyalty.

I believe two steps are needed to develop this layer of loyalty. First, decide what positive characteristics you want people to display in your workplace. ACX Transportation, "Where the safe drivers work," would say the company wants safety-conscience drivers. The second step is to be the mirror and tell employees when they are demonstrating that positive characteristic. At ACX, managers could tell drivers that they see them as being safe operators, if they indeed are. So you need to define what type of people you want to have working for you, and then reflect back to the workers a positive projection of that image when they perform. Although this may sound simple, finding such characteristics in a workforce obsessed with diversity makes this a real challenge.

When we bred our dogs, we used a designer theme, a red poodle with a blonde golden retriever. We convinced ourselves and those adopting our puppies, that our dogs were a super-breed. We named each pup after a designer, and we explained the benefits the goldendoodle breed brought to their family. People saw themselves as smart, exclusive dog owners who would be the envy of their friends and family.

The same can be done at work. Begin by helping people believe they are part of a special group that others wish they belonged to. Select an admirable attribute for people to identify with and convince the workers to believe it about themselves. Provide ways for and encourage employees to act on the positive image. If the leadership of ABC Electronics states, "Where ideas are welcomed, watered, and rewarded," ABC must follow through by setting up a suggestion box or holding an idea contest with a meaningful reward.

When you reward employees, the reward should be tied to the positive attribute of the company. You must communicate your image and keep it fresh with new posters, new statements, and a scheduled presentation of information pertaining to the attributes you want your employees to project. A great image can become stale or tarnished if left alone for too long, but if the main idea behind your reflection is noble, it can last for a long time.

I once worked for a division of the Volvo Corporation (who make trucks and diesel engines along with many other industrial products). While traveling, we used a Volvo credit card with the Volvo logo and wore Volvo outerwear. I can't tell you the number of folks who spoke to me and the other employees about their Volvo cars, how much they loved their vehicles, and how safe they were. Numerous people gave me an in-depth description of an accident they were in while driving their Volvo and the positive results for having purchased the safe Volvo car. Volvo had a reputation for building high-quality, safe vehicles, and people assumed that those of us who worked for the company knew a great deal about cars and safety. The world-recognized Volvo image started with the Swedish manufacturer's vision that vehicles should be built with a deep and primary concern for the passengers' safety and protection, making safety the predominant focus of the firm. I was working for the finance arm of a company with a seventy-five-year image that had never died.

If you want to develop an image for your company, you must start with a predominant purpose. Is it safety, speed, reliability, or something else? Pick one thing that you can be the best in doing, make everything else subservient to that purpose, and the world will recognize your employees as people with a special purpose and image. Do not underestimate everyone's need for an image in their work; you are to your workers the mirror and the makeup artists all rolled into one.

Midlevel managers can reach employees with powerful image builders. One of the most powerful ways to boost employee image is to find ways to make your worker's image shine with value and significance at home. I once worked for a vice president of sales who sent my wife a beautiful basket of roses for Christmas each year to thank her for her supporting my efforts on the road for the company. When we entertained people over Christmas, our guests would ask my wife whom she had received the beautiful roses from, and she would tell them, "My husband's boss sent them to me." Give employees something to boast about at the neighborhood cookout or holiday party. By making them look good in front of their family and friends, you deepen their loyalty. Anything that you can offer your employees that enhances their image and tells the folks at home that they are valued members of the team creates an image that will make people want to work for your company.

I believe Americans have such loyalty to their dogs because their dogs make a silent statement in their homes. The dog sends a message about who its owners are to everyone who enters the home. Employers and managers who send a positive image into their employees' homes tap into the same stream of loyalty.

CHAPTER FOUR:
WHAT DO I DO? THE PURPOSE GAP

"Many hands make light work."
—Irish proverb

IF YOU'VE HAD THE OPPORTUNITY to play a backyard game of football with a group of young children, you may recall handing out assignments in the huddle. You explain that John will hike the ball to Sam, and before you can tell Sam to throw the ball to Pete or Pam, one of the children immediately asks, "What am I going to do?"

Everyone wants a role and to be part of something greater than themselves. The human spirit is wired with a need to know that the work we do serves other people and makes a positive difference in people's lives. Work was once known as "vocation" or "calling," in which the labor, whether paid or unpaid, contributed to the greater good. The need to realize our purpose remains, though it may be difficult to comprehend in many modern vocations.

The unfulfilled need for purpose provides leaders another loyalty opportunity.

As we met with families that wanted to adopt a dog, we saw that these families wanted to be a part of something. People adopting dogs weren't looking for a task, such as feeding and training a dog; they wanted a role with a purpose, a desire to participate in something significant for their family. Some people came with the purpose of filling the emptiness resulting from the loss of a family dog, while others wanted to give their children a loving companion. People wanted to be part of something important, whether it was healing a hurt or making a dream come true. People like to feel that they are doing something that will be remembered. The same desires follow people to work, and in those desires lies another opportunity to build loyalty.

The word "partnership" is often used in the workforce; it means to have a part, a role, just like a part in a play. The desire to be part of something is a deep emotional need that people are looking to fill in many ways. You'll often hear sports fans say about a team for whom they do not play, "We beat the Omaha Mud Slingers." The word "we" is used instead of the stating the team's name because of the need to be part of something.

The families adopting our dogs were participating in and adding a major chapter in their life stories. We provided the opportunity to add purpose through the adoption process. Owners later shared with us the dog's new name and how they liked the dog, along with reports of special events they had experienced. The notes and updates about the dogs were simply accounts of the families' new roles regarding the dog chapter of their lives.

A workplace can leverage the same human desires by moving from an exchange of money for labor, to creating a story that provides roles for people to play out. Everyone wants to be part of history, and your followers desire to have a key role in your company's story. Most companies talk about the founder on a Web site or brochure, and people want to know about the origins and who started the business. However, I'm convinced that workers need to know their part in the company story to feel like they belong. Managers who can identify their employees' roles within the company's story will build deep loyalty. Telling the company story and including employees' names and roles fills the gap between feelings of insignificance and feelings of purpose.

During a business meeting, managers typically discuss numbers and results without providing names or stories, often ignoring the importance of who did what. Managers who can shift the quarterly numbers report to a quarterly narrative that includes names and roles will see an immediate difference on the audience's faces. If a pro athlete tells the story of a championship game that his or her team won and only speaks about his or her role, you're turned off; if he or she simply read the box scores and statistics, you'd be bored. However, you are endeared to those who name their teammates and describe the significance of each member's role. The same holds true for business meetings with your group—don't forget the color commentary about the players.

Sporting events and news shows that give members of the crowd a chance to be on television inspire people to bring signs, stand in line, and endure all sorts of weather just so they can have a part. My daughter was attending a bowl game in which she and some of her friends were featured on ESPN; they were able to wish the television audience, "Happy holidays," and shout, "Gig 'em, Aggies." She received a dozen text messages from friends saying, "I saw you on TV." It was about being part of something big and, for a brief moment, being in the show. The old saying that we all get our five minutes of fame is about our desire for purpose.. This is part of the gap that a manager must help his or her employees fill in building loyalty.

The major networks aren't likely to send television cameras to your office, but you can close the purpose gap by helping employees understand what they do, why it's important, and how it impacts the organization and its customers. When leading a compliance business, the workers were involved in what most folks would consider boring, unglamorous work of keeping trucking companies' paperwork up-to-date and legal. It was easy for workers to build large gaps between who they were in significance and who they wished they were. Attitudes always turned positive when we reminded the various workers about the significance of keeping twenty-five thousand truckers on the job by having up-to-date paperwork that allowed them to operate and keep the distribution system of our regional economy moving. When you stand up and tell people in front of their peers that what they're doing is important, you help fill the gap. The better you understand what your workers do and how it contributes to the company—and to a greater extent the economy—the greater the impact will be.

A simple set of actions to leverage this loyalty button requires managers to think and present information like a narrative, as opposed to a box score. Managers must remind those they lead about the importance of each role. In doing so, you keep the purpose bucket in your workers' minds filled.

Chapter Five:
Can I Count On You? Commitment

"Hope deferred makes the heart sick."
—Proverbs 13:12

THE BRIDGE OF LOYALTY IS hard to build, however keeping it open may be equally difficult. Have you experienced times when workers, who you had known to be loyal and cooperative, suddenly become argumentative and resistant to change? Have you had people that after many loyal years of service begin to push back toward leadership? Behavioral changes from loyal employees may be an indication that the bridge of loyalty is in need of repair. Sometimes this kind of change reflects skepticism or doubts that the employee senses in your commitment to their success. People tend to doubt the dedication levels of their managers and leaders. Employees need reassurance that managers are dedicated to a plan of mutual success. The container of assurance that allows an employee to remain faithful to his or her manager and invest their loyalty has a tendency to leak when doubts as to leadership's commitment occur.

When the families came to pickup their puppy, the response of the pup left no doubt in the new owners mind as to the dog's commitment to his new family. Each puppy wagged their tail, kissed the owners face and curled up in their arms. While nobody expects their manager to respond like a puppy, many employees see the relationship with their boss more like a traffic officer, sitting at the bottom of a hill, radar gun pointed, ready to hand out a ticket. Employee doubt as to leadership's commitment to them and their success can be damaging to performance.

Set up a speed trap and people start to drive below the speed limit. Act in similar fashion toward workers and productivity slows.

The sports world in recent years has demonstrated the significance commitment can play in supporting a bridge of loyalty that leads to mutual success. Robert Kraft, the owner of the New England Patriots, effectively communicated his commitment to his players" success, which resulted in an unusual response. When the New England Patriots introduced themselves in Super Bowl XXXVI as the New England Patriots with no individual introductions, sports fans applauded, and the team went on to win three championships. In Super Bowl XL, Pittsburgh Steelers player Jerome Bettis, known as "The Bus," played for a smaller salary late in his NFL career for the chance to win and retire a champion. Several players on the 2006 NBA Champion Miami Heat played for similar salaries and reasons. The veteran leadership on these teams inspired individual loyalty and dedication to the mutual success of the team. Commitment that motivates loyalty involves personal effort to achieve a common goal or purpose, not just a personal return. The sports world has also shown the weakness that occurs when commitment is replaced with selfishness and manipulation. When a first-round pick dedicated only to his own salary goals, fails to show up for training camp, the team and player typically fail to achieve a winning season. We see shameless self-centeredness in some veteran players, whom fans disdain. Most of us would have no interest in watching a spoiled, selfish athlete negotiate for more money. Fans want to watch the magic of unselfish teamwork coming together to accomplish a shared goal.

Transferring these ideals into the workplace is not easy, but is critical to long-term loyalty relationships. Commitment is the employee's belief that you are placing part of the company's success on their efforts and ability, providing the necessary tools and support promised. It is where obligation and duty are fulfilled, managerial promises are kept, and responsibilities are remembered. When commitments are fulfilled, they are like rods of steel strengthening the bridge of loyalty. When managerial promises are neglected, structures are weakened, doubts are aroused, and the gaps begin to appear. Unchecked doubts leave your workforce vulnerable to offers wherever they sense commitment levels are stronger. The weakening of loyalty from the perspective of commitment might be broken down into the categories of obligation, fickleness and expectation.

The starting block for eroding employee confidence in leadership's commitment is obligation. Employee confidence is eroded with one broken or one perceived-to-be-broken promise at a time. For the most part, my three daughters had consistency in their babysitting jobs for family and neighbors, but occasionally they found themselves with broken commitments. These included last-minute cancellation and the group outing with a multiple-family pay plan that paid the single-child rate. The message sent in these babysitting scenarios was a no obligation message in regards to the sitter's time. A "no obligation" message can also be sent in adult work settings. Employees can feel they were shorted time during their lunch hour or worked late without compensation. Employee incentives and bonuses are promised in the interview, but aren't paid. A lack of obligation can bring about violence, as was the case in 2006 when a truck driver shot and critically wounded his supervisor in Fort Worth, Texas, over his pay. Commitment doubts will occur anytime a no obligation message is sent. If you promise new tools and did not provide them, you in turn send, the no obligation message. When repeated no obligation messages are sent, the employee enters into thoughts that are toxic to loyalty. They don't care why should I becomes the question in their mind.

A second difficulty in keeping the commitment message from leaders to employees strong is the occasional fickleness of people. Managerial politics facilitate employee fickleness that can create a shifting loyalty and cause damage. The political arena is a great picture of this fickleness. The Democratic presidential primary contest of 2008 was one of the most interesting political races in modern times because of the fluidness of voter commitment. It seemed that each time a candidate won a primary or group of primaries and began to pick up momentum, the voters' support seemed to switch to the other candidate in the next big primary. The shifts in political support followed a path based on doubts aroused by candidates' negative attacks on one another. Organizational shifting of loyalty in complex reporting systems often happens for similar reasons. The same kind of fickle support can take place in a workforce with internal turf wars, dedication to department heads, and negativity. Businesses where employees report to different managers are prone to the same shifting loyalty seen in political races. Retailers are prone to this problem as crews report to the manager on duty, let managers take on the same kind of political rhetoric and negativity toward one another, and the fickle loyalty of politics is likely to follow. If two department heads complain to their direct reports about the other department head a puncturing of employee assurance will take place followed by mistrust. When managers speak negatively about one another, the employees may question what the manager thinks about them. This impact of fickleness like that seen in politics should be simple to avoid. Simply observe a political debate, and never act in a similar manor to one another as managers. When a manager has an issue with another manager, settle the matter privately and never discuss it with employees.

Like many relationship problems, expectation is a major contributor to the weakening of the relational structure. There is nothing like an unmet expectation to undermine the foundational strength of loyalty. Human expectation and understanding about how the give-and-take is going to work, and who will do what, can move from misunderstanding to gossip to hostility. Expectation is where the weakening of the commitment begins because it allows people to justify the pulling back of their loyalty. Businesses are also prone to a time-and-favor exception axis. The longer people are in business, the more favors that will be asked of one another, and many are outside the original terms of agreement. Favor begets favor, and before long, the agreed-to give-and-take looks nothing like the original terms. If one person is more aggressive or manipulative with strong influence, it's a matter of time before the less aggressive person feels he or she is being taken advantage of, resulting in erosion of devotion to the business.

The first step in strengthening the commitment gap of loyalty is to ask each person if he or she believes in the relationship. This may sound trite, but the trusting relationship of marriage begins with a statement of vows as a sign that each person believes in the principles of the relationship. We asked families if they were committed to our values when it came to dog rearing. We were not asking people to agree to an unreasonable list of duties and inspections, which we saw some breeders demanding, but we absolutely asked folks about their commitment to our values. I'm convinced that discussing your values and seeking a verbal commitment better serves the relationship, rather than simply signing a corporate values pledge.

The second component in the strengthening of your commitment message, involves the detection and prevention of erosion in the relationship. In the summer of 2007, most people saw the horrible bridge collapse in Minnesota and the tragic loss of life that resulted. The tragedy was the result of failed inspections, repairs and maintenance, and work relationships require similar prevention processes. Relational maintenance is easy to ignore and rationalize away as unimportant and insignificant. Leaders need to ask themselves have I kept my obligations, did I mislead anyone's expectations? In 2008, a Philadelphia bridge inspector double-checked a small crack on a bridge on Interstate 95 and may have prevented a repeat of what took place in Minnesota. Relational cracks that seem small in terms of obligation, confidence and expectation should not be taken lightly. Business leaders need to be visible and schedule personal interaction with employees to discover relational cracks. During these interactions, you may discover erosion points and can then begin working to keep things together. Who is bored, who needs more of a challenge, and where might people be feeling taken advantage of are discovered in interaction. Exit interviews are often too late to identify erosion in preventing turn-over, but can be used to identify relational issues that need to be addressed. Managers must use caution in exit interviews, do not assume that because the person is no longer working for the company that everything said is valid and truthful.

The bridge of loyalty also requires commitment guardrails for it to function correctly. My wife and I agree that money is the cause of many marital problems, so we agreed early on that neither of us could spend more than $300 without the other's consent. Should my wife or I veto the other person's $300 item, the one denied was not permitted to be angry toward the denying party. Neither of us asked too often for this privilege, and neither of us frequently said no. This simple agreement kept us from financial erosion of our relational commitment. Business leaders and employees have common erosion factors that can ruin a business relationship. Common points of erosion include employee responsibility, benefits and company policy. Businesses often prepare extensive employee hand books to cover weather, funerals, sickness and a host of items that act as guardrails in preventing favoritism or unreasonable actions. Managers can prevent tragic bridge departures by knowing and using the manuals.

Finally, define what commitment looks like in terms of your business, and then celebrate commitment results. For example, a trucking company could start by explaining in a meeting what it wants people to be devoted to in terms of goals and actions. The leadership might state that it expects drivers to commit to delivering on schedule. Leadership defines how the goal is achieved by measuring the number of on-time deliveries and follows up by posting the percentage of on-time deliveries. To demonstrate to the drivers the company's commitment to the goal, a stringent vehicle maintenance program is implemented, telling each driver they are being provided a dependable truck to succeed. When the company reaches the goal, the leaders should declare that everyone has won and celebrate the accomplishment. The company can throw a celebration the way a professional sports team does with a party, T-shirts, and fanfare. I had a friend whose company celebrated the year-end accomplishments with a theme; all the employees received a T-shirt, theme related buttons, and awards. The event acknowledged and rewarded the team in a celebratory manner. One year the theme was a marathon, as it had been a long and difficult year that ended well but had not been easy. They gave everyone marathon runner type shirts, and then ran through the streets of Dallas and handed out metals to everyone involved. It sounds corny and weird, but it worked in building commitment to one another and reassured employees that management still believed in them.

Commitment must be sought out early in a relationship, and the core values and components must be written and reviewed so each party can be reminded about what was committed and what was not. Commitment review is as important as performance review, as you will find very few people perform well, while at the same time holding serious doubts as to the leadership's commitment to their success. We live in a fast-paced business culture in which everything, including job descriptions, changes rapidly. The frequency of an annual review is not sufficient to keep loyalty from eroding. Leaders must take the time to periodically insure that the commitment message supporting employee loyalty is in tact and strong.

CHAPTER SIX:
CAN WE TRUST EACH OTHER? CONFIDENCE

"If a leader pays attention to lies, all his workers will become wicked."
—Proverbs 29:12

THE ECONOMIC DOWNTURN IN 2008 involved a chain of lies and breaches of trust in both the mortgage industry and the investment firms that sold the mortgage investments to their clients. Applicants misstated their income and mortgage brokers failed to check references and the validity of the applications, while investment firms sold the mortgages to investors as low-risk investments. A chain of deceit forced the Federal Reserve to provide billions of dollars to prevent a collapse of Wall Street—an unprecedented move—while billions of dollars were lost along with thousands of jobs. The lies created the largest government bailout in the nation's history at a cost that will take years to determine.

The amazing part of placing dogs with families was seeing the immediate trust that people appeared to build with their puppy. The puppies picked the owner more so than the owner picked them, and a trust in the relationship began from the first day. A family must trust the dog in their homes and around their children, and from the emails we received the initial trust we witnessed has not been broken. Dogs are thought to be protectors of our home, companions to our family, and for most dog owners trusting in their pets is often easier than trusting in people. The trustworthiness of our pets is in most cases a faithful adhesive that holds the relationship together.

The second support beam holding the bridge of loyalty is trust. Deceitfulness, real or perceived, can crush the loyalty of your employees like the mortgage fiasco, causing collateral damage throughout the business. Trust can be destroyed with incredible speed and ease in our electronic world. Trust, like commitment, is essential to loyalty, but it is different in that commitment is concerned about the company's willingness to place the weight of its success on the worker, while trust is concerned about the employee placing the weight of his or her success on the company.

A man I know told a story about his second-grade grandson who, unlike George Washington, managed to create a whopper of a lie. The man explained that because his grandson's handwriting was not up to the teacher's standards, the little boy was placed in a tutorial class, which the boy viewed as a stigma. The second- grader got on his mother's computer and sent the teacher an e-mail explaining that his handwriting had improved and that he no longer needed to attend the tutoring sessions. The teacher sent the mother a reply via her e-mail to verify it was really the mother, but the little boy managed to intercept the message before his mother received it and replied with a confirmation. The teacher decided to look into the matter with a phone call, and the second-grader was exposed.

The story illustrates the ease with which we can deceive in the electronic age. Unfortunately, in the area of loyalty, such behavior is catastrophic. In our world, a person's confidence and reputation can be destroyed electronically in a matter of minutes. If something unfavorable is discovered in the office, the e-mails and instant messages circulate with unprecedented speed. Today's communication methods also allow for slow, subtle erosions of trust when people read into e-mails; someone sees hostility or negative feelings that the sender doesn't specify or intend. The ability to inject a false assumption into e-mails can have a freeze-thaw effect that can crack the trust that supports loyalty. The art of verbally and visually seeking confirmation that a listener understands the speaker's message in a conversation is lost in e-mails and text messages.

The old sender-receiver model of communication is difficult to use with today's technology-dependant workforce. The difficulty in electronic correspondence is not just an issue of good communication;

it is a matter of trust. Every time someone acts on a misunderstanding and has to be corrected, you erode trust between the person who had to be corrected and the person who provided the message.

Employers today may set up corporate witness protection systems out of the fear of litigation and allow accusers to remain anonymous, leading to increased suspicion among middle management. The fear of legal action has set up employees to be like neighbors who call a protection agency on a parent they think is abusive. In companies, the employees are reporting on what they think is a manager's inappropriate behavior. You can debate the merits of an anonymous process when it comes to children, but such processes in the workplace may cause unwanted gossip and assurance erosion. We see trucks with 800 numbers that encourage motorists to call and report an unsafe driver without giving a name. Customers can fill out anonymous satisfaction reports on service employees. The impact of all the anonymous chatter can create an atmosphere of mutual distrust. The news media reported that Vice Presidential candidate Sara Palin did not know Africa was a continent, according to anonymous sources. It was discovered some time later that the anonymous source was a hoax, a campaign advisor that did not exist. The media had not checked the factualness of the story. The effect for many is a distrust of what they hear from the news.

During the summer of 2008, the three-year-old colt Big Brown attempted to make history by winning the Triple Crown. Although he failed, his failure reveals the ease with which we break trust in business. Big Brown had won decisively in the Kentucky Derby and the Preakness Stakes, so when he finished last at the Belmont, fans and the media began to assess blame. Was it the jockey or the trainer? Was the horse on steroids? Sometime later a photo showing his loose shoe solved the mystery. Human nature demands to know who committed a wrongdoing, and trust requires that we suppress that desire and find out the facts.

One of my responsibilities as the Business Leader, while working for the Road Manager division of Volvo Finance, was to manage the money that our firm took in for our services. We had deposits on hold in an escrow account that needed to be tracked and reconciled, but had been neglected for several years. I was challenged to fix the escrow account and establish better policies to monitor the account.

I hired a retired finance manager to reconcile the account and put in a process to keep it reconciled. He was making tremendous progress and had developed a plan to get our accounts in order. He had the finance skills, and I knew where to direct him in terms of the business and how things worked.

My immediate supervisor called one morning wanting me to investigate why the balance was so low in our escrow account, according to the morning bank statement. He wanted to know where the money had gone, and he wanted an answer now. I was receiving e-mails hourly in all caps demanding that I fix the problem or explain the balance. (Why do people believe that by using capital letters the problem will be solved faster? I'm sure the person reading the e-mail is thinking, "I'd normally ignore the problems of my company that I am paid to fix, but those caps are terrifying! I'd better get busy.")

My finance manager and I were perplexed by the low balance, but we knew something had to be wrong in what my supervisor was seeing because we had kept track of deposits and disbursements and did not see any significant gaps.

Upon further investigation, we discovered that the corporate treasury department swept any balance over $100,000 out of the account nightly, making overnight deposits for interest and redepositing the money in the afternoon. My manager was unaware of this action because he had only seen the balance prior to the redeposit. He calmed down after we informed him that the gaps were caused by the treasury's actions, not us.

It became apparent to me how fast I would be blamed for anything that went wrong financially and I would need to prove my innocence or be presumed guilty when it came to money. The blame first, investigate later mind-set did not bode well for building trust.

My company was later purchased, and another a similar scenario occurred with the new company's COO. The chief operating officer was reviewing our account activities after midnight and mistakenly identified a cashier's check for a check made out for cash. We used cashier's checks because some state agencies required it, while checks made out for cash were prohibited. Before the new leadership discovered the mistake, e-mails flew around the organization, and my new manager pointed her electronic finger at me, demanding an explanation as to why

I had requested a check for cash. No one bothered to review the item in question or view a copy of the check; nor did anyone apologize for accusing me of breaking company policy when I had not done so.

When this type of "prove to me you're not a thief" attitude is assumed, employees tend to place less loyalty in the relationship. This type of reactive, accusatory fire prevents employees from growing their loyalty. Leadership needs to learn to ask questions, such as, "Please help me understand what happened here?" Retailers face this situation regularly when the cash registers are counted and are out of balance. The key is to get the facts with carefully chosen words and make sure you have the facts before you accuse someone of something they may or may not have done.

Trust is most often tested when things go wrong, not when things are going well.

You must first decide that employee trust is an important value. When crisis management is called for, ask yourself if any trust issues could arise from the way you handle the employees involved. Second, managers need to realize that if people really want to cheat the company, they typically will do so in small ways that go unnoticed, not by actions that cause a crisis.

Trust involves one person placing the weight of his or her reputation and success, in some degree, on another person. A hiker crossing a rope bridge of planks paints the picture. If you step on the first board and it cracks, you're not likely to have confidence in the boards in the middle. The same is true in terms of business. If you crack under the first crisis, assuming your employee acted foolishly or did something that will hurt the business, without giving him or her the benefit of the doubt, you are the first board that cracks. It may be possible to crack and apologize, so long as the next incident does not repeat the behavior. Leaders who arrogantly ignore these scenarios will not build the trust needed to deepen loyalty.

Managers establish trust by clearly defining the principles the company follows, consistently communicating to employees those ideas, and acting on those precepts. Every business will face changes in its operating conditions, but the underlying principles for which the business stands must remain consistent. It is hard to build trust in a flavor-of-the-day structure.

Employees' trust is most often eroded by their immediate supervisor's words and actions. By following a few basic rules, managers can prevent the toxic words that eat away at trust.

First, do not ask an employee questions that you do not need to know the answer to. It's like having children away at college; you don't need to know everything, so don't ask about those things that are embarrassing or personal. If your company provides paid time off, do not ask an employee why he or she needs a day off; it is something the employee has earned. If you have specific days or seasons that are not vacation-friendly, make it a policy that no one can take time off during those weeks, or at least communicate the seasons that you require all hands on deck. I had a supervisor who would, in her mind, jokingly ask people why they needed a day off. People were intimidated by the joking and found it offensive; some lied because they felt they needed a medical reason to get a day off.

Secondly, for those tasks involving money, create tools that force accountability, so a tool is the policeman, not the manager. Use automation for everything financial, such as expense reports, banking, cell phones, mileage allowances, and time sheets. When you invite an employee into a discussion regarding misuse of money, the employee is on the defensive. Managers should use great care in conversations involving money and should completely research the concern before the conversation. Advise employees that they are being monitored, thereby removing the temptation to be dishonest. Use the right tools to catch those who are cheating without offending the majority who are not. Someone once said, if you expect dishonesty, you'll never be disappointed; it will happen. When it happens, the offending employee must be handled in a way that doesn't cause greater damage to the trust within the organization. Therefore, leadership's resentment toward the dishonest worker must be subdued to prevent mistrust among those who are trustworthy.

Third, take the time to ask your workers if they feel mislead about anything regarding your business relationship. With all the electronic communication in which body language and tone are removed, people can read into items an attitude that was not there or not intended, creating a belief that they've been mislead. Taking the time to inquire about how the workers see the work relationship going in terms of trust may short-circuit misunderstandings.

CHAPTER SEVEN:
WHAT SHOULD LEADERS EXPECT? OPPORTUNITIES

"Go to the ant, you sluggard, and consider her ways and be wise."
—Proverbs 6:6

SO WHAT SHOULD LEADERS EXPECT for their efforts to cultivate and strengthen loyalty?

Leaders should expect more effective employees, lower administrative cost involving the workforce, and more time to dedicate to improving the overall business. The new buzz phrase *engaged employees* being heard at many conferences discussing human resources, may best explain the benefits and opportunities of loyalty. The term engaged, describes a workers sense of connectivity to the company, many new studies are reporting on the benefits of *engaged employees*. As you might expect *engaged workers* are less likely to leave than non-engaged workers, and some reports suggest *engaged employees* file fewer grievances, spend fewer days on workers compensation when injured and simply are less costly employees. Some studies have reported store locations with *engaged employees* sold more merchandise than similar stores with fewer employees described as engaged. Leaders should expect a reduction in employee cost, better attendance, a more productive worker and the precious freedom to lead.

The movies *Eight Below* and *Iron Will* tell the stories of dog sled teams, and both films portray two benefits that every business and organization needs to succeed. The dogs' loyalty to their owner enables the sled to be pulled forward as each dog runs in the same direction according to its position. It may seem cliché, but it tends to be the biggest challenge every business faces as it grows: if only we could get everyone rowing the same way. The second benefit, as seen in *Eight Below*, is portrayed by the dogs' ability to survive in extremely harsh conditions. Loyal work teams can both propel a business forward and, at another point in time, survive difficulties and stressful situations. You need loyalty the most when your business hits a rough spot; that characteristic can be the difference between survival and failure. The intense loyalty between the dogs and the men that drove the sleds in both films created the opportunity to compete, and the adhesive that held them together in difficulties.

We saw similar benefits of unity and survival as part of the experience people saw in our dogs. I am sure the families that adopted our dogs like most families probably do not agree on what toppings to order on their pizza, but when it came to the dogs the unity and agreement among couples, children and families was amazing. The families we dealt with demonstrated a willingness to move forward in unity, as they saw their new puppy's loyalty to them. While the people who adopted our puppies did not sign any of them up to pull a sled, several opportunities were made possible through the loyal relationships that were built by the dogs and their new owners. One mom in particular, was concerned about her daughter who was away at college and sometimes became a little homesick. College kids can often slide from homesick to depressed and the mother did not want to see that happen in her daughter's life. She took a chance and gave her daughter a puppy to take back to school as a companion. It was rewarding to hear some months later from the mom, the puppy had cured the homesickness and had made her daughter's time away at school more enjoyable than ever before. There were others who came to us to adopt a dog because it had been a dog that had helped them through tough times, and they expressed to us the desire to have a similar relationship in their life should hard times and difficulties come again.

One of my favorite parts of college football is the halftime show involving the marching band. The band and its leaders paint what every organization desires: everyone marching to the same beat, playing their musical part, and following the directions while the paying customers watch their musical formations. After leadership has built a bridge that provides a path from where employees are to where they want to be with trust and commitment in place, amazing achievement happens. This is when those in charge can take their team onto the field and perform.

When leaders attempt to direct the enthusiasm fueled by fidelity and commitment into the organization, they need to keep in mind a few simple realities regarding the human condition.

Remember that people tend to follow winners, passionate personalities, new trends, and uniqueness. We all want to be a winner and associated with winning. Copy bands follow successful bands with numerous hit songs. Teams that win the Super Bowl, World Series, or any championship of notoriety suddenly sell more team merchandise and have a larger fan base. We want to identify with charismatic personalities because they often express what we feel.

The good news for businesses is they can define what it means to be a champion. Leaders can be a big personality within their respective company, though they may not be to the outside world. A business can proclaim itself or its product as the newest trend with some substance to back it up. And all organizations are already a unique group with certain characteristics that when identified and communicated can allow people to think of themselves as special.

Start by defining winning and what your company or group must do to attain the title of winner. Present people with the definition of winning, provide a vision of how this can happen for them, equip them to succeed, and then get out of the way. Post your gold records and ribbons on the wall and tell them about the hit songs you're selling as a company.

People tend to follow big personalities or leadership styles. Once again a business can define the style of leadership it wants people to follow. Leaders should start by asking themselves, "Who am I the leader, following?" Once you determine who you as the leader are following, you can introduce your leader to your followers, providing the followers an opportunity to better understand your leadership. If the copy band follows a famous band and most pro athletes emulate a superstar they admire, then you as a leader must find and define who you are following. Bill Parcells has mentored numerous coaches in the NFL and many of those coaches follow his methods. Most of the current NBA superstars follow Michael Jordan, and business leaders are no exception. It may be that you follow Jack Welch, Warren Buffett, or Bill Gates. I once worked for two gentlemen who quoted Jack Welch; I read Jack's book and implemented some of his ideas. My immediate supervisors and myself were all following Jack's methods and ideas, and we deepened our loyalty to one another and the company because we were following a set of principles that we all believed in.

The benefits of a faithful workforce that is sincerely committed to the company's advancement are countless, but the two that matter are the funneling of work in the same direction and survival ability when the storms of business roll in.

Chapter Eight:
Who Else Should Join the Team? Recruiting

"But a faithful man who can find?"
—Proverbs 20:6

COYOTES RUN IN PACKS BUT send just one member when they hunt for prey, including small dogs. One coyote will attempt to entice a small dog into a chase game that results in the dog being led astray and destroyed by the pack.

Unfortunately careless recruiting involving just one member can be devastating to a workplace and the team. After you have bridged the gaps, established commitment and trust, and have a loyal following, you are vulnerable to new recruits. You want to avoid hiring employees who may lure loyal members of your team into destructive thinking. When this happens, it ruins the efforts you spent so long building.

The best way to keep a positive culture in your workforce is to recruit people who are wired to be loyal. My daughter Katy and her girlfriend were in my home having dinner with my wife and me. I suggested to Katy that she didn't need more girly men in her life, but rather she needed to find some manly men. Her girlfriend asked me, "Where do you find them?" I love that question in any context because it cuts through the obvious and gets to the need for real answers, not just slogans or sayings.

Most businesses are aware of the challenge to keep their culture strong when adding staff. Managers want to hire loyal, dedicated employees. The question is, where do you find them? If we could only state with certainty that people from a certain town, college, or military branch would solve the problem. Some people appear to be more dedicated than others, and that characteristic is difficult to uncover. Unfortunately, the workforce interview process typically fails to go beyond experience and skills, forcing managers to make an educated guess or surface observations about a character issue that lies deep. Interviewees are coached on what to say and what not to say, so it should not surprise managers when the person selected in the interview is nothing like the person on the job.

While my wife and I were attempting to place our puppies with families, people's loyalty was obvious and plainly revealed. People entered our home naturally relaxed as we invited them into the kitchen to look at the puppies. We sat around the kitchen floor with families, chatting about their life and needs. I am convinced that the setting you choose to interview folks and your ability to help them relax are key in discovering their dedication. It is unlikely that interviewees will open up and reveal deep emotional characteristics in a stiff, formal venue. It is reported that Warren Buffet takes people to a family-style restaurant in Omaha and orders everyone a root beer float. This is the kind of atmosphere that people relax in and one that needs to be facilitated in the interview process if you want to get below skill set, experience, and appearance. It is what Karl Rove and other political advisers call the kitchen table issues, the things people care about. In the interview process, it is the place people tell you what they care about.

The first and most prevalent characteristic of loyalty I observed among the dedicated dog adopters was the motive for which they came. It was always more than just their own needs or desires. Some folks came because they wanted to give their children a happy experience; others came to help a family member replace a pet. All of them were there to serve someone other than themselves. Knowing why the person is interviewing is critical. Is it just about them, or do they aspire to serve others in the office or serve the industry or sector? Interviewers should try to determine whether there's a greater motive in the applicant's desire for the position.

One of the crazy parts of placing the pups was the length of time people spent in our home. Total strangers and their kids often spent two or more hours with our puppies and us. This experience showed another revelation about loyalty traits that should be sought in recruits. Simply determine if they are patient. Committed people are not in a hurry to get through the interview process. Patience is an easy test of loyalty that you can readily observe in the interview process. If you have folks who are reluctant to make a time commitment to you in the interview process, it may be an early warning of commitment issues after the hire. Nobody says, yes, I will marry you, after meeting for five minutes. Most people can't order lunch after viewing a menu for five minutes. So it should raise a red flag if the job candidate is in a big hurry to get it done. Shallow commitment leads to resentment within a group, followed by friction, conflict, and eventually disloyalty.

A third observation that is difficult to uncover in an interview, but is a clear sign of loyal people, is the willingness to learn. If a person keeps telling you he or she is a good learner during the job interview, interviewers are likely to think the candidate is an idiot, or at least unqualified in terms of the needed skill sets. Instead, people tend to tell you what they know and downplay their willingness to learn. A teachable spirit, however, was dramatically obvious in the families adopting the dogs and different from anything I had observed in the interview processes in business. My wife would explain crate training and the type of food we used, and without exception, people thanked us for taking the time to show them information and usually asked additional questions. We gave them e-books and details about the breed. People eagerly accepted our offers, and no one who adopted a dog looked at us like a student receiving an unwanted homework assignment for the weekend.

I suggest as part of the interview process that the interviewer show the candidate something that he or she is unlikely to know from reading the company Web site, and observe their response. How the person responds will tell you the individual's willingness to learn, but also how important the job is to the person. If you are serious about something and someone begins to explain things to you, you have no problem listening. You typically ask questions because you want to know more, and you almost always thank the person instructing you. If you don't care deeply about a topic, you simply nod your head politely and maybe provide some halfhearted thanks.

The last observation that is relevant to the interview process as managers attempt to recruit loyal workers is the excitement factor. In one adoption, a dad was so excited to give his son a puppy that he and his wife started Christmas a week early. He said his son couldn't read a calendar, so why wait? The overall tone of the prospective new dog owners we met was similar to the excitement people show before going on vacation or attending a big game. How excited is the candidate interviewing for the job? Do they follow up with a phone call or e-mail? Presenting a professional appearance and staying calm may be what we're all told to do while interviewing, but excitement about a job is often a sign of loyalty. I realize the fire can die for a hundred reasons after the honeymoon, but not having it in the first place only leads the new hire to dissatisfaction more quickly.

Baseball has two types of leagues: the majors with the best players, and the minor leagues, whose players are in need of improvement because they can't play well enough for the majors. Getting a chance to play in the majors would bring excitement to the minor league athletes. I'm also sure that all aspiring players are willing to learn what it takes to play in the majors and maintain their patience to get there.

When recruiting new members who you hope will be loyal, find a setting where the candidate can relax and look for motive, patience, willingness to learn, and excitement as clues to measuring the candidate's future dedication.

CHAPTER NINE:
WHAT ELSE CAN I DO? VOLUNTEER LEVEL

"A volunteer is worth twenty pressed men."
—Unknown

FRED SMITH PUT IT THIS way: "Leadership is getting people to work for you when they are not obligated." [4] Interestingly, his company, Federal Express, is headquartered in the Volunteer State of Tennessee.

The volunteer sprit is the deepest sense of loyalty an organization can achieve. The volunteer spirit is not a culture in which people work for free, but rather they freely offer information, ask for more responsibility, and provide the extra effort that would otherwise mean adding staff or hiring a consultant. This scenario occurs when employees deeply believe in the business and want to help it advance. They are generally willing to contribute at a greater level because the company fosters an atmosphere of freedom of thought and expression. These companies encourage feedback, solicit ideas, and give credit and praise to those whose ideas and efforts help advance the business. The volunteer spirit is hard to ignite and can be quickly extinguished by careless managers.

My wife is a dog lover and has met most of the dog owners in our neighborhood while walking our two dogs. She routinely volunteers to watch other folks' dogs because she truly enjoys dogs. One of these dog-sitting jobs illustrates what managers should not do if they want to develop a volunteer level of loyalty among their staffs.

One summer my wife met a young woman who had rescued a dog and was about to head out on a vacation with her husband. My wife volunteered my youngest daughter to care for the woman's dog while she was away for eight days. The woman and my daughter agreed to a fee of $10 per day.

On the first day of their vacation, the husband called and asked if my daughter could bring in the mail and papers, a service not originally requested, and she said yes.

The first couple of days that the dog was with us were decent, but he began to bully our dogs and would not leave us alone. On the fourth day of the dog's visit, my wife and daughter placed the dog in our backyard with our dogs. My wife soon discovered that the dog had eaten through our fence and had run away.

She began to search frantically for the dog in our neighborhood. Fortunately, my wife found the dog within a few minutes because a service man had put him in his truck. The man had called the owners, who, of course, didn't answer, so the man left a message. My wife took the dog to his owner's home, and while trying to get him out of the car, she closed the door on her hand. She soon wished she had not volunteered for this duty. My wife and daughter then decided to leave the dog at his own home, and they faithfully fed and watered the dog.

My daughter, seeing that the dog was a bit destructive to the owner's home, put the dog in the fenced-in yard on the day the couple was returning because she was concerned he would tear up the house. This was not a good decision with the Texas heat being high, but the dog had been shaven, had plenty of water and shade, and seemed to do better outside. My daughter was watching another family's dogs at the same time, and they were fine with the dogs being outside.

When the owners returned home, they heard the message from the driver of the truck regarding their dog's escape attempt, and they assumed the worst about my daughter and us, not realizing the dog was lost for only a few minutes. They were also unhappy that the dog was outside when they returned, even though they had not left instructions as to their preference.

In the end, the dog was fine, the house was fine, and considering there were no instructions, it went well. Everyone in our house was glad for this event to be over because the dog was not very well trained. The fence-eating dog's owner, however, was irate that his dog was not inside and was furious that we had not contacted him about the escape, even though the dog was not harmed nor had it been out of the yard for long. The couple said they were so upset that they were willing to pay only half of the fee they had agreed to. When the man of the house finished grilling my daughter, he offered her $40, instead of the $80 he had agreed to pay. We were appalled because we knew the truth, not just an assumption. We refused the $40 payment, expressed our frustration, and left.

This incident is unfortunately what many employees experience at work. Employees are appalled when an unsatisfied manager who provided no expectations or instructions scolds them because the worker didn't read the manager's mind. Managers who pile on work not stated in the original agreement, and those who assume the worst about an incident fail to get all the details, and then play the paycheck card are too common in many business settings. They act like the neighborhood cheapskate mentioned in the story. In that case, the dog owner had just saved himself hundreds of dollars by not using a kennel. The dog-watching saga lays out exactly what *not* to do if you want a deep spirit of loyalty that pushes your employees to go beyond their standard job duties to exist.

If you want people who are willing to volunteer for jobs, sit on committees, or participate in any extra effort task, you must keep the employee's motivations, skill sets, and perspectives in mind, and be appreciative you have people with a deep sense of loyalty to your leadership. Carelessness with people at this level of deep loyalty is risky, because offending them will result in significant set back, both in their loyalty and with others. People will think, look what happened to Charlie after all he did, I am not going to make that mistake, and will simply meet the requirements.

First, be careful about piling on the work when it comes to those who are willing to go the extra mile. Managers tend to ask those who they know will say yes when additional work must be done. Managers cannot fail to give instructions and details of their expectations, fail to inquire about the status of the task, and then be super-critical of the results.

Although an employer would be taken to court for the "I am paying half" approach, I've seen employers that have refused to pay employee expenses or sales commissions, as well as countless contract employees who have been compensated unfairly. Shorting a worker will always result in killing loyalty, and in some cases, may result in violence in the workplace. One of the biggest complaints among owner-operators in the trucking business is settlement pay, because it involves the amount owed for hauling the load minus advances for fuel, tolls etc. One of the biggest problems for restaurant help is being cheated out of the tip share if one exists. This may sound contradictory to what is written about money, but it is not only the money at issue; it is the manager's accusations behind it, or the tone and choice of words used in resolving these types of disputes.

Managers must consider perspectives that are different from theirs. If a worker with a different perspective of how a job should be done completes the job with the same results, the manager should accept the completed task, instead of beating them up about the details of the process. In the case of the neighbor's dog, my daughter had cared for the animal; when the owner returned home, the dog and house were in the same shape as they were before the couple left on vacation. When this type of thing happens in business, pay the employee for the completed job and adjust the details the next time if you feel them to be important.

If you want an employee to follow specific instructions, you must use the printer and paper when delegating a task. Do not assume that everyone shares your ideas about how something should be done. If an employee doesn't perform the task to your satisfaction, ask yourself where you failed to communicate before you beat up a worker over your disappointment.

Managers also need to ask questions when an incident occurs. If the employee was putting forth extra effort when the incident happened, be more flexible about the results. During a football game, a receiver who fights for a few more yards will more likely be involved in a fumble than the receiver who steps out of bounds with each catch. If you start your questioning by insinuating that the employee was acting foolishly or stupidly, your anger and frustration will kill the spirit of giving extra. Statements like, "I am really disturbed by what I heard from our accounting department about you. Please explain …" implies that you believe the accusation. It is a guilty-first approach that's sure to kill the volunteer spirit.

Workers are motivated to do more when you clearly communicate what you want them to achieve and then celebrate their achievement when they make it. Find the positive progress, appreciate the extra effort, and be slow to find fault. When things go wrong, first find out what role leadership played in the problem, and then find out what tools or instructions would have made the task easier to accomplish. This approach may sound soft, but even in cases in which an employee simply neglected his or her duty, you may find the person who failed more willing to admit the mistake and take corrective action if you're slow to accuse.

Finally, managers should understand that conflict is unavoidable, regardless of what you do, and conflicts can sabotage your efforts of maintaining a volunteer spirit. The spirit is often ignited by detailed cooperation and accomplishment, and it is extinguished when conflicts are left unresolved. Make every effort to resolve conflicts between leadership and those who follow. Conflict resolution is a process of hearing each side without interruption, seeking trusted counsel about how to resolve the issue, and striving for reconciliation. Sometimes respectfully agreeing to disagree may be all you can do, but having aired the issue allows the spirit of loyalty to continue.

Conclusion

"A wise man will hear."
—Proverbs 1:5

MARK TWAIN ONCE SAID, "THE more people I meet, the more I like my dog." If you owned the mother of our puppies, you might agree with the statement, but if you owned Beurré, the father, you likely would not agree with Mr. Twain's assessment of humanity and canines. However, most people recognize the wit of the statement if they have been a leader of people. Managing people and motivating them to pledge their loyalty to your leadership is difficult, for many reasons. Leaders will be best served by focusing their efforts on the best employees instead of trying to fix the bad habits of the few.

Beurré, the father of the puppies, was a drain on our energy because we found ourselves constantly repeating commands that we thought he understood. He was not a stupid dog; he simply had no desire to understand our commands and wanted only to be in charge. His stealing a turkey leg on Thanksgiving made it easy for us to give him away to a lady who managed a pet store and loved poodles. She was aware of his obstinate nature and was okay with it. Yes, we had a turnover situation of our own. It is the same way in business. When either side refuses to try to understand the other, relationship issues and breakups occur. It wouldn't be fair to leave you with the impression that turnover is something that should never happen or is always a negative event. Sometimes letting people go is part of the loyalty solution.

There will be times when managers will have to make difficult decisions. Loyalty focused leaders will struggle with decisions involving layoffs, discipline, promotions and raises, concerned that their actions might negatively impact loyalty. There will be times when leaders will wonder if their motives and decisions are the right thing to do in terms of loyalty. The canine relationship offers insights in examining leadership decisions and loyalty.

One might say the difference between good dogs and bad dogs is determined by the dog's effort and willingness to understand the owner. When a dog seeks to understand and follow the owner's commands, most owners reward the dog with treats and extra efforts to please the pet. In the same way, employees distinguish between good leaders and bad leaders by the leader's willingness and efforts to understand the employees' needs and desires to close the gaps in their life through their work. In the same manner, the manager who truly seeks to understand his or her employees will often find his or her following responding with extra efforts to help accomplish the business's goals. The Scottish preacher Allistair Begg, once spoke about the difference between manipulation and motivation. It might be paraphrased for a business in the following sentence. If you as a leader are influencing your workers for your good it's manipulation, but if you influencing your workforce for the good of your company it's motivation. I would add that if you influence people for both the benefit of the business and the good of the workforce you will build a loyal nation.

In the early part of this writing I listed three popular leaders that many people look toward, to close the gaps in their lives through politics, spirituality and pragmatic advise. The managers who can help people see work, as the means to filling the voids of privilege, image and purpose, will build strong loyalty. Work is in many ways a better means to filling these desires, and a healthier track for people to chase their dreams. Seeking to understand people's privilege, image, and purpose gaps is the key to accomplishing a loyal workforce. A manager will spend less time navigating through turnover and recruitment if he or she makes an effort to relate to the worker. Managers who seek to understand will often hear fewer employee complaints as a volunteer spirit begins to catch fire. Managers who often describe their role as babysitters or glorified hall monitor will be freed up to focus on advancing the business because less time will be needed to monitor and settle grievances. The events that drive managers crazy will decrease in frequency when the right understanding is established.

In this book's foreword, I referred to an article in *Workforce Week* that had reported that the turnover rate at Starbucks among store managers was 20 percent and for employees was 80 percent.[5] Compare those numbers to the quick-service food industry's turnover rate of 200 percent. Starbucks fills its workers' gaps of privilege with things like a free pound of coffee and free in-store Internet access. The employees also gain an image of someone hosting a cool place to hang out and the cool skills of a barista, all while working with the purpose of providing people a unique coffee experience. The loyalty at Starbucks, in my opinion, is much deeper than screening for personality traits, pay, and benefits. Starbucks success has to do with hitting many of people's loyalty buttons and creating a workplace Where employees see being there as a means to closing the gaps.

St. Francis of Assisi wrote a famous prayer that requests divine assistance in being able to understand people, as opposed to being understood. This is the essence of *Doggone Loyalty*. It is a guide to understanding the nature of human loyalty among those who follow you. The prayer goes on to say that it is in the giving that we receive. Leaders who give time and effort to understanding their followers' needs, will in return receive their loyalty.

Endnotes

1   Frederick F. Reichheld, *Loyalty Rules: How Today's Leaders Build Lasting Relationships* (XXX: Harvard Business School Press, 2001) ###.

2   Gretchen Weber, "Preserving Starbucks Counter Culture," *Workforce,* February 2005, www.workforce.com.

3   Joel Osteen, *Become a Better You: 7 Keys to Improving Your Life Every Day* (XXX: Free Press, 2007).

4   Fred Smith, www.heartquotes.net/Leadership.html (accessed 2008).

5   Weber, "Preserving Starbucks Counter Culture."

www.ingramcontent.com/pod-product-compliance
Lightning Source LLC
Chambersburg PA
CBHW021020180526
45163CB00005B/2046